LOVING YOURSELF INTO BEING

Feb 15, 2021

Dear Amber,

Congratulations on winning!!
I am so glad we're now connected!
Your journals are gorgeous ☺. I hope
you enjoy these poems and that they
can give you some rest during your
studies!

Warmly,
Tarini

LOVING
YOURSELF
INTO BEING

KARINA HSIEH

Cover Illustration by Leslie Bodner

ISBN: 978-1-7346143-0-5

To all the souls who have been, are,
and will be Love in form.

"What is the heart? A flower opening."

—Rumi

Hello Friend,

Thank you for holding these pages within your hands. They contain vast amounts of Love that I hope will accompany you on your journey through life. This is **your** adventure, so you're welcome to read these poems in any order, all at once, or one or two at a time. You can flip around or go by section — whatever catches your fancy.

I wrote the three sections — LOVE, BECOMING and MIRACLES — with the intention of displaying various aspects of Love and cultivating your own self-love and compassion so that you awaken to the magic within yourself and your life.

These poems are here for you any time you want to feel loved or remember your own deep capacity for compassion, kindness and Love. They are designed to dance playfully across the pages to bypass your brain and nestle into your heart.

I hope you always know that you are enough, exactly as you are. Right here, right now, and always.

Together, we are loving ourselves into being.

With Love,
Karina

Table of Contents

PART II — BECOMING

PART III — MIRACLES

PART I
LOVE

Self-Love Earplugs

These two fluffy puff balls are for you
to nestle into your glorious ears.
To protect you from the static,
the insidious buzz of gossip,
vile words that sting your eardrums,
and pollute your heart.

Collect yourself in your inner sanctuary—
your spacious cavern fortified by peace—
illuminated by laughter.

Insert your earplugs anytime you want
to mute the raging world,

to dissolve

c o m
    p
     l
      e
       t
        e
         l
          y

into your own symphony of love.

The Green Thumb of Love

Self-love is the water that blossoms the soul.
When our souls are shrouded
with self doubt and judgment,
shriveled up, a husk of themselves,
we must nourish them with our own love and kindness.
We must embrace our bodies,
the shelter of our souls with open arms,
our limbs draped around ourselves in a cocoon of care.

Let your body know it is safe,
it is loved,
it is whole.
Pepper your soul with sprinkles of joy,
mist it with compassion,
kiss it with kindness.
You water every other soul,
fluffing up your friends,
sharing how wonderful they are.
Why not water your own soul,
your best friend for life?
Cherish yourself,
and you'll bloom into your full glory again.

Love Beams

Light the candles behind your

eyes,

So you can send

B
L   E
O   A
V   M
E   S

to others.

Dear Heart

Thank you for your patience.
I am getting to you,
my sweet, sweet heart.
You have waited,
with every beat
for me to remember
that you love me unconditionally.
I have for too long bumbled around
searching for other hearts to love me,
but you are my most essential heart.
You are my greatest love.

Watercolor Love

Your love washes over me
in waves of watercolor:

Lavender,

Baby blue,

Orange,

Pink.

Each kiss feels like a paint-dipped brush
dotting a speck of water,
swirling its lovely hue
in the expanding drop on my body.
Every kiss layers itself over the others,
creating a rainbow across my entire being.
Adorning all of me with your love.

Darling

Oh darling, you aren't like us.
You glide on this earth like it's heaven,
treading on clouds,
while the rest of us bumble on soil.
You see rainbows when others see storms.
You see goodness when others see guile.
You haven't yet been conditioned
towards apathy like most humans;
you still acquaint yourself with angels.
Please never lose your luster,
your shiny, golden Love —
your alabaster aura,
gleaming with goodness.
Guide others to seeing
the likes of Heaven on earth —
to create their paradise here, now.

M
O   N
O

that we're gazing at the same

And remember,

P
U

just look

When you miss me,

Missing Me

Heartbreak

A cannonball collides with my heart,
obliterating it into a million pieces.
My lungs are about to collapse from a lack of air,
squeezed by an iron clamp.
I'm attempting to breathe underwater,
but my lungs can't hold the liquid.
There's a numbness in my belly,
that chilly void between disappointment and devastation.
To not be the one loved.
To not be chosen.

I breathe deeply into my heart, lungs, belly.
There's a cavern of sadness dwelling within my rib cage.
Grief crashes over me like roaring waves at high tide,
pummeling my bones,
pelting my lungs with ice,
splinters knifing into my flesh.

Breathe.
        B r e a t h e.
                B   r   e   a   t   h   e.

Loving Yourself Into Being

I embrace the pain.
I feel it deep within my organs,
deep within my bones.
This pain shall pass.
But for now, I hold it in reverence,
for it reminds me that I am truly and completely alive.
Oh the depth of our feelings!
It's such an exquisite life —
that we can feel this rainbow of emotions,
anti-gravity highs and sea-floor scraping lows.
And yet, we breathe, we love, we live.

Inhaling deeply into the left side of my body,
I embrace the excruciating pain,
knowing I have loved harder and deeper
than I ever thought was possible,
that my capacity for love is vaster
than I could have ever imagined,
that I'd conjured up false edges to myself.
This pain is a portal to push past the old walls of love,
so I can love even deeper in the future.

Loving Yourself Into Being

Our hearts are so resilient.
They shatter and yet remain completely intact,
healing invisible slashes with scars to love again.
Fill up that maelstrom of strife with fresh oxygen,
fresh thoughts,
fresh compassion.

We are living big, full lives.
If we didn't love with our whole hearts,
if we never experienced heartbreak,
how could we grow our hearts
even bigger, stronger and more loving?

Like any muscle,
our hearts break and build up again.
That is how we get stronger —
how we become even more
loving versions of ourselves.

Love & Soul

Oh sweet darling, leave an ounce of love for yourself;
don't ooze it all out lest you have nothing left for you.
Nothing to spare.
Nothing to give.
Your love soothes the soul,
heals all the cracks in your shell,
in your spine,
in your center.
It aligns your chakras,
nudging them lovingly,
so that they whir and hum gently,
spinning in unison.
Replenish your own fountain of love.
Drink from your well your own divine, delicious elixir.
Heal yourself so you can heal the world.

The Water Balloon of Love

You toss the squishy, blue balloon
between two lovers —
filling the space with an aerial arc,
a rainbow span of love.
Catch and release the balloon,
not too hard or it'll break;
not too light or it won't carry.
The perfect toss to make safe passage
into the cupped, open hands of the other.
Lovingly embrace the orb once it lands.
Let it rest a second,
before catapulting it back
for the next vault.

Full Heart

I've been
sweeping the rooms
of my heart, wiping away cobwebs
from the corners, decorating the walls with pretty
paintings, tidying it up for my loved ones. It's been a
wonderful home for me. I've relished sleeping in every
groove, dancing my heart out with every beat, and fill-
ing it up with song. But after loving my heart fully for
one, I am ready for even more affection to overflow
these halls, creating a joyous home for many.
Who wants to join me in this beautiful
nest I've made? I'm ready for my
rightful roommates—the ones
who will light up my
core and brighten
up our entire
world.

Puzzle Pieces

Our souls clicked like puzzle pieces,
fitting perfectly for a glorious moment.
If only time could ooze like molasses,
trickle like water in a drought,
to better savor this essential second.
And this one!

But nothing stays the same.
Nothing lasts forever in this sweet embrace,
this intoxicating union.
Relish the time with your loved ones.
Cherish every chance you get
to build these sacred connections.

One day, we will all disentangle ourselves
from the puzzle,
returning to rest collectively in the puzzle box.
Yet each of us will never be the same
after the magic moment when we clicked.

The Nectar of Love

Drink the nectar of love with cupped hands

until your veins course with honeyed gold,

your body shining with pearlescent bliss.

The Weight of Love

A bowling ball

P
L
U
M
M
E
T
S

to the bottom of my belly.

I can hardly breathe.
Can you wait, Love?

Oh, the
WEIGHT
of love.

I yearn for you to stay,
to postpone your float to heaven.
I am human after all,
leading with a lead-laden heart.

Am I selfish for anchoring you to Earth,
forcing you to reside in an ever-more aching body?

Oh, the weight of love....

Do you wait, Love,
or become weight

                            l

                               e

                                 s

                                     s

                                         ?

Us

Where do you end and I begin?
Like the ocean caressing the sand,
we flow in and out of each other,
in waves of hi's and bye's.
Our edges have melted into one another,
like the colors blending in the rainbow,
our souls bleeding into one.

The River of Love

I stand knee deep
in the River of Love,
running my hands
lovingly through the
flowing rapids. "What
are you doing?" queries
my curious companion
standing on the riverbank.
"I'm dancing in Love! Why
don't you come join me?
Anyone who partakes is
in Love with me too!" "But
I thought you could only love
one person at a time? And you
and I are just friends, so would
that not be weird?" "Love is the
river—it flows around us as long
as we decide to wade in it. We can
be in Love with anyone and everyone.
Most people only allow one person to join
them in the river, romantically, but the truth is
that our capacity to love is infinite. All of our past
lovers can choose to stay in Love with us, even if our
dynamic has changed—they don't have to return to shore.
That is how I choose to love unconditionally, by staying in
this river. To be in Love with everyone." My friend ponders
this for a moment, slips off his shoes, and frolics in Love too.

Shooting Stars

Two shooting stars
glimmer in the night sky.
Close enough in orbit
to almost collide,
to revolve for a second.

For a moment, time stands still.
These heavenly orbs freeze in a shimmering dance,
reflecting and relishing the other's presence.
The Universe undulates outward,
expanding to envelop
a multitude of planets, galaxies, milky ways.
And yet, simultaneously,
it shrinks to the size of an atom.
A tick in time elongates into eternity —
infinity, and yet collapses into itself.
Into Now. Now.
NOW.

If only time could stand still.
Two shining hearts beating as one —
shimmering for two,
lighting the sky on fire.

A lightning bolt strikes.
"Crack!" *Thunder*.
A burst of flame.
The clock strikes midnight.
The second hand ticks.

Ahoy!
These shooting stars restart their engines,
resuming their individual tracks.
Only a molecule apart,
yet a world away.
A moment in time of bliss —
pure connection,
                    unity,
                              love.

A quick embrace.
A glance.
Recognition.
A slight head bow.
'Til the next celestial dance.

Orbits

You choose your orbit,
and I'll choose mine.
We can dance around each other
but never lose our center.
If one of us should pull too hard
that would be the end of us.
So keep your dance,
and I'll keep mine.

Let Me Hold You

That which is a burden to you
is a gift bestowed upon me,
to help you,
hold you,
love you.

Like Yin and Yang,
you flow into me as I flow into you.

Worlds Apart

Darling, we were meant for two different worlds.

Mine is on the side of sunshine —

yours on the side of moonlight.

Neither is wrong.

We just crave different aspects of the sun.

Missing

I miss you like frosted, minty breath
inhaled into my heart,
leaving a chilly cavern.

Puzzle pieces gone

missing.

Sand Castle

We built our love with cups and crests,
molding sand into a beautiful castle fit for a king.
Using shovels and stones,
I fortified it thinking it would last,
but you knew the waves would crash,
sweeping our home to sea.

Alas, nothing remains forever in this protea world,
but at least we had a few moments of bliss.
Those will be forever harbored in my heart —
the most permanent of residences.

Echoing Love

What is that feeling?

Love —

      echoing through each chamber of your heart,
      reverberating against its walls,
      magnifying more and more with every moment.
      Pulsating through your body,
      it expands until it floods every cell,
      every fiber of your being,
      until all that you are is

                          Love.

Falling in Love

Love is when your heart expands so much
that your rib cage can't contain it.
You simultaneously breathe lightly
to prevent your heart from popping
and also fill your belly deeply
to anchor you into this world,
lest you float away with giddiness.

Love is when you're bursting at the seams
with overflowing joy,
liquid honey oozing over your edges,
bathing your body in a glistening, golden glow.
You become a fountain of happiness.
Like a sponge,
you grow w i d e r and w i d e r ,
soaking up this wondrous water.

Loving Yourself Into Being

You beam a rainbow smile,
one with a jackpot at both ends
and a massive toothy highway to connect them.
Every cell in your body tingles,
trembling from the intensity
of your newfound love.

Like a rumble of the earth,
waking up your heart from its sleepy slumber —
you are fully alive.
Your skin dissolves as you dive headfirst
into this enthralling river of love,
not caring if you ever resurface.

Synergy

We are not two halves that make a whole.
We are two complete souls.
Two cups overflowing into a third,
generating more than you or I alone.
What else is this but magic?

Mirror

I am a mirror for you,
           just as you are a mirror for me.
    I am held
        and can hold;
    I am seen
        and can see;
    I am heard
        and can hear;
    I am felt
        and can feel.

My emotions are my own,
and yet are one and the same as yours.
My heart, while housed within my body,
is threaded to yours —
inseparable in spite of space and time.

Our hearts beat as one,
our breaths as one,
our thoughts as one,
our purpose as one:
    to Love
        and be Loved.

We create separation,
differentiation from one another out of fear
that we are not enough,
that we cannot be loved,
that we do not deserve
to be on this physical plane.
We have forgotten our true selves,
our highest selves,
that can only BE loved
because we intrinsically are just that:
Love.

It is not about being worthy or deserving.
It is within us innately,
residing in every cell of our being,
flowing as naturally as the oxygen
that glides in and out of our lungs.
We have just forgotten.
Thus, I am here
to remind you of your true self
in your fullness,
in your glory,
in your wholeness.

I must reflect back to you
the essence of your being,
which is the essence of mine.
Love. Love. Love.
You are Love.
Only Love.
Completely Love.
Forever.
Love.

Loving Yourself Into Being

PART II

BECOMING

Loving Yourself Into Being

Yin Yang Bodies

Like Yin & Yang,
we are part light, part dark.
But our world trains us that only our
light is acceptable, that we must shun our
darkness to be loved. We leave our shadow
side behind, locked up in a prison in ourselves,
only loving half of us. But our darkness should
not be feared or loathed— it builds bridges
of compassion and empathy for others.
By embracing our other half, we
become full, inspiring
others to love all
aspects of their
stunning
selves.

The Atlas of Our Minds

We constantly etch the geography of our minds,
expanding into new corners and grooves,
exploring crevices and ravines
that we didn't know were there.
We think our atlas is permanently etched,
but our mental terrain, our brain's tectonic plates,
continuously shift, lift, and coalesce.

When an earthquake happens,
one that rumbles our personal
beliefs, that is the perfect time
to pioneer into new lands.
Rather than cower in a
corner of our minds,
clinging to the old
rubble, we can charge
ahead to seek fresh
vantage points —
to observe the
novel landscape.

Curiosity
leads us into
a new reality,
one that could
entirely upend
our prior ecosystem.
From flat to round,
our world has shape
depth, polarities.
One's North is South.
One's Summer is Winter.

When we hit a rut,
we can flip our mental globe upside down,
gaining a fresh perspective —
a new opportunity to move forward.
This constant re-evaluation helps us refresh
our mental model from outdated maps,
ancient perspectives that must fall away
like a snake's desiccated, old husk.
From there, we can explore our new world
with open eyes, open minds and open hearts,
ready to sketch in the next frontier.

Holding Up the Sky

I sat on the bank of a river,
wearied from a long day of hiking.
A black raven perched on a branch above me asked,
"Hello friend, why are you so tired?"
"I'm tired because I've been carrying
the weight of the world on my shoulders
so others can be freed from the burden.
It's exhausting and lonely up here."
"No wonder you're exhausted," mused the raven.
"That isn't your job.
Did you ever think that by shouldering
the burden of humanity, you're making others small?
You need to let them hold up the sky.
And then it won't feel so lonely either."

With those words, the weight melted off my shoulders
as a lightness blossomed in my being.

Yes, I need to let others hold up the sky too.

We Are Whole

We are whole, complete and perfect
just the way we are.
We are David in a slab of marble,
having caked on mud around ourselves
until we think we're a block of mud,
not a perfectly polished, priceless piece.

We think we're unworthy, broken, commonplace, dirt,
but we must chisel away everything that isn't us —
stories and beliefs we had conjured up out of fear
until all that is left is

US

as we have always been:
whole, complete and perfect.
Perfectly and utterly
Love
inside and out.

Wrapping Paper Bodies

Our bodies are wrapping paper.

We get so distracted by the wrapping

that we forget there is a present inside.

Windmill

Rather than let the wind knock

y o u d o w n ,

Become a W I N D
         M I L L

and use that force for fuel.

Brain Wash

De-clutter your mind
like you clean your house.
Sweep out the extraneous facts
littered across the grooves and corners.
Wipe away cobwebs from cherished memories,
golden moments you'd long forgotten.
Tuck them into your souvenir box
to reflect upon at any time.
Clear out old files of information,
numbers no longer needed.
Retain the good moments;
release old, unwanted stories.

Make it squeaky clean.
You're creating space for the new —
experiences and feelings that will make you glow.
Breathe deeply into your cleared mind-space.
You can now enjoy dwelling in your own brain.
This is your home, to love, create and cherish
all moments that are, have been, and will be.

Turbulence

Turbulence in the mind,

SK
I
D
D I N G

from thought

to thought...

Buckle up.
S l o w

d

o

w

n.

It'll be a smooth ride again soon.

Breathe in.

Breathe out.

The thoughts will quell.

Thick, grey clouds
thinning
into light wisps of

m   i   s   t

Brain Fires

There's a fire burning in your heart,
in your soul, in your mind.
Quell the one in your mind
so you can magnify the one in your heart.
Your brain has been whirring too fast,
worrying about silly nothings —
scared to die, yet not actually living.
We all have a terminus,
an end to this current corporeal experience.
Do not worry about the end;
just live in this.
Present.
Moment.

This one!
Not the one in your head pondering the future.
If you look only at the mountain top
while you race ahead on the trails,
you will trip on the rocks at your feet.
Bruised and battered,
you'll pick yourself up
just to blindly run to your destination.

Slow down into your present —
tread softly —
actually seeing the little pebbles,
the white daisies on the wayside.

Then, and only then,
are you actually living,
actually here.

Thank your overworked mind.
Let it relax off the treadmill,
hop into the hot tub, and soothe itself.
There is nothing to fear,
nothing you are missing.
You have everything you need,
right here, right now.
You are here, you are here, *you are here*!

You are breathing, reading these words,
loving a little more with every heart beat.
You, my friend, are enough;
you have always been enough.

Just continue to breathe,
and with every breath,
send a little more love into this world.
Open your heart,
let your head rest,
and receive the soothing elixir of life.

Umbilical Cord

Every moment, I am tugged forward
by an invisible umbilical cord
leading me toward my future.
It tugs at me like an eager hunting hound
sniffing out rabbits,
guiding me to victory.
Like a wind pulling the string of a kite,
my cord lurches me forward this way and that
as I traverse the windy path up my mountain.
I follow it blindly, faithfully,
knowing it will
never lead me astray,
never asunder —
only to fulfill my wildest dreams.

Kintsugi Hearts

Dear Broken Heart,

You will mend with liquid gold

c
    a
       s
          c
       a
     d
      i
       n
         g

into your crevices,

making you stronger,

brighter

and more beautiful than before.

51

Use It All

We use what is important to us.
While dancing,
we thoroughly use up the dance floor,
utilizing its space to share moments with others,
to dance our hearts out,
to live each moment fully.

While living,
we ought to use up our hearts
like we have 4 or 5 of them,
not holding back any of our love for later.
All we have is this moment.

Let's use up all of our hearts,
to make this one precious life burn bright.

Edges

While bats use sonar,

We use

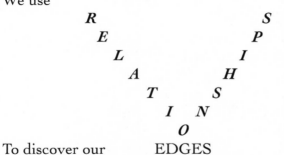

To discover our   EDGES

So when someone challenges your perspective,
thank them for helping you better understand yourself.

Twinkle Lights

We are souls tightrope walking
across crisscrossing, twinkle lights —
twinkle lights that undulate up and down
from trellis to trellis.
Our bodies sway gently
in the light, balmy, calm night air.
The smell of the salty sea breeze
pricks our nose,
a little dash of pepper
to spice up the evening.

We look down at our feet,
high above the rolling grassy knolls underway.
A thousand feet high,
yet not an inkling of fear in our minds.
We balance on this rope with ease,
having navigated this thread day in and day out.
Our center engaged,
we intuitively lean in or out based on each step.
It is actually harder to navigate the ground,
when one is so used to light walking;
we have air legs on land
after walking on wind currents for so long.

The instability reminds us of our lives,
how every second is another step
into the unknown.
We cherish and seek that unbalance,
that wavering, rocky feeling,
as it makes us feel alive,
appreciate the moment,
drink in the beauty —
the essence of this world...
This ephemeral world
that can dissolve in an instant,
when we blink, when we close our eyes.
That darkness —

Were we asleep for a minute,
an hour, a day, a lifetime?
When our eyelids shut
and our bodies fold into sleep,
time stands still.
It elongates and shrinks simultaneously,
like the undulating twinkle lights
that can stretch for miles,
yet tucks itself gently into a small embrace,
a tiny circle wrapped around itself.

That darkness is not to be feared;
the unknown not to be cursed.
They encourage us to feel with our other senses,
expand our comfort zones —
our current physical boundaries
that have yet to be tested.

We need darkness
to deepen our gratitude for the light.
When we open our eyes
to see the trail of glowing ants below our feet,
their luminescence at first
is almost blindingly bright,
but then our two gleaming orbs adjust.
Ah yes, sight.
We can see again
as we do every moment,
every day...

Or do we?
Are we still in the same lifetime,
as we had been the second
before we had closed and opened our eyes,
like a clamshell under the sea?

Loving Yourself Into Being

Are we awakening from a dream,
or had that been a continuation
of our reality before blackness?

We are twinkle lights —
a tiny bulb that blinks to darkness,
that awakens to light,
that threads on to black,
then back to the light,
continuing up and down in space and time,
connecting with each other here and there,
before we continue down our own individual tracks.
Continuing in this light grid,
until we all reunite at the end of the trellis.

Building

Invest your love, energy, and resources
into people and experiences,
for Nature does not appreciate diamonds or dollars.
In a fire, all buildings burn.
In an earthquake, all cities collapse.
So build your relationships,
decorate your mind with memories,
for those, Nature cannot touch.

Concerns Caddie

Did you know
that you're a

c
o
n
c
e
r
n
s
  c
a
d
d
i
e
?

Day by day you pick
up a golf ball or two
of concerns from others
and tuck them in your bag.
You wonder why your
back hurts, why you feel
so weighed down. Those
are not your concerns,
my friend. Take off your
bag any time and release
your concerns, Caddie.

Molting

You are a phoenix rising
from the ashes,
from the dust.
Like a snake shedding its old, molten skin,
you shake off your former shell,
your old self,
the one that you have outgrown, outlived.

You are like an oyster
with some nagging piece of grit swirling,
sloshing around your mouth, gargling,
roiling over and over
until it lathers into a gleaming, pearly sphere.
You spit it out,
admiring something that once was so despicable,
now transformed into a treasure —
a jewel, refined and lovely,
polished from years of hardship.

Like an orange spotted butterfly,
you emerge from your caterpillar cocoon,
unfurling your nascent wings from the shadows
into sunlight.

Loving Yourself Into Being

Like a newborn baby,
you open your eyes,
blinking in the cool air,
so fresh and arid after the warm waters
you've bathed in your entire experience.

You blink again,
looking down at your new evolved figure,
your powerful red plumage.
You tense your muscles,
flexing new wings,
gathering strength,
gaining power.

One last clench —
you push your talons against the ground,
launching yourself into the air,
shedding the last film of soot off your belly,
off your entire radiant being.

Home Body

Our body is our home.

Let us stop creating a shelter with

booby traps, prisons, and dark corners.

Light it up with love.

Open the windows to refresh the soul.

Floating Thoughts

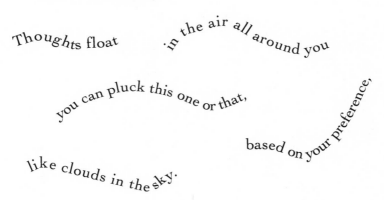

Thoughts float in the air all around you

you can pluck this one or that,

based on your preference,

like clouds in the sky.

Each thought has a frequency.
High vibration ones feel better than low ones.
So spend time with people whose frequencies soar—
their energy will make you feel bright and warm.

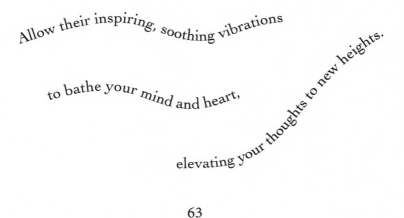

Allow their inspiring, soothing vibrations

to bathe your mind and heart,

elevating your thoughts to new heights.

Curtains

The shimmering silver curtain
sashays in front of me,
obscuring the doorway.
Do I enter into its chambers?
Do I cross this liminal threshold?
Or is it better if I remain here,
a place I already know?

This side is comforting.
Although the air surrounding me
is stagnant and stale,
it is all I have known for a while.
It isn't oppressingly stifling yet
so surely it can't be all *that* bad?

Like a rock in a riverbed,
I have lain asleep
in a long stupor,
urged by the currents
to tumble downstream,
yet weighed
          down,
               by my own stubbornness,

sluggishness, lethargy —
to stay in this one, singular, secure spot!

I know this niche —
it suits me well;
why fix what isn't broken?!
But is a hovel still a good one,
when squatting there ultimately
buries me deeper and deeper
into the ground?

Do I pull myself out of this shallow pit,
or allow the waves above
to push me down into this hole that I, myself,
have selected passively
by not objecting,
by not rejecting,
by not shifting?

If I were to actively uproot
from this knowing place,
and tumble, fumble
through the waves down the river,
would I find a better home?
A nice place to reside?

Loving Yourself Into Being

Would it be an oasis or hell-hole?
Inaction is an action, a choice,
and I am being shoved,
deeper and deeper,
into my current depths,
as I contemplate my next steps...

Yes, I will head downstream;
I will step through the silver curtains.
It is better for me to dive into the unknown,
into the depths of the abyss,
for staying here will ultimately be the death of me.
For if there is no growth, no change,
how am I truly living?
What will be my evidence
at the end of the day?
Better for me to cascade ahead,
downstream and into new walled rooms,
to discover fresher water, fresher oxygen;
to re-ignite my lungs and heart,
which have for too long
been quelled into submission,
silenced by the stillness.

So I step forward,
my hand brushing aside the silver beads
hanging down from the doorframe.
They hug me in a welcoming embrace
as I enter,
as I unfold,
into this entrancing, new frontier...

Tightrope Walking

You balance on a tightrope,
arms outspread for balance.
Belly tight, chest up.
Now is not the time to look down.
Set aside your fear of heights,
or any dread of falling.
You go where you look,
so look straight ahead.
Lead with your heart.
Your feet will follow,
just as they have every step until now.

One heartbeat, one step,
One heartbeat, one step.
Trust your soul;
It knows what to do —
It always has
and always will.

Connect the Thoughts

Connect the thoughts

like constellations in the sky.

Each nexus, each node,

flows into another—

weaving a tapestry of ideas,

cultivating a brain map of new creations.

Candle

I am a candle.
My top edge morphs into a deep pool
as I near my flame.
The closer I lean into my glowing crown,
the harder it is to discern if I am the candle
or a liquid pool of wax.

I am one with all,
both solid and liquid in form.
My head is hot, aglow,
a puddle of burning thoughts and desires.
The rest of me is rigid,
fixed in this body as I am,
or so I believe.

I am hot and cold simultaneously,
fluid and structured,
glowing, red, and pale.
I am fire.
I am powerful.
I am cool.
I am strong.
I am tall.
I am everything.

I, the candle,
burn until I am nothing at all.
Just a trail of smoke in the wind,
burned bright into the ether,
dissipating back into...

My shell heaps in a pool on the ground,
a cloak of my former self,
a mask of my being,
releasing my essence to the world.
One day I'll be reshaped,
molded into another beautiful candle,
to light up the world anew.

Darkness

You walk down the corridor to a closed door.
You turn the cool, bronze doorknob,
opening the door inwards.
There's darkness on the other side,
a black hole of nothingness.
But this is not scary; you were born out of nothing.
Your first 9 months of being were in darkness;
this is your home.

Dance in the darkness.
Revel in your quiet sanctuary
where you can just be —
completely yourself.
No need for a mask.
No need to hide.
No need to care about your outer hide.
No labels or externalities.
Just....
                    You.

Embrace the Rain

Embrace the rain.

It is the Universe's sign

that you are not alone,

for it weeps in joy

and sorrow for you|

washing away your pain

and refreshing your soul.

Frolicking in Nature

What greater joy is there than frolicking in nature?
When leaves dance down from trees,
floating effortlessly on airstreams?
The crackling crunch of crisp leaves underfoot...
the playful splash into a raked leaf pile.

What bliss to play lightheartedly as a kid again,
to make snow angels in leaves,
arms and legs waving up and down
like wiggly cooked noodles.

Sitting on a see-saw,
riding up and down,
feet bouncing off the ground,
flying in the air for a few seconds.
Oh to be a kid again!

And yet we are always kids;
youth is a state of mind—
a label we attach or detach at will.
We can peel off our self-prescribed labels
like layers of an onion.
The old, desiccated film
plastered to our surface unravels
revealing fresh layers of shiny purple and white!

To be a big kid with a big heart,
eyes as huge as saucers,
seeing the world with wonder.
We have a sweet tooth for knowledge;
our brains eagerly anticipate
new streams of information
like syrup drizzled over a pancake,
soaking it in —
until every particle is sopping,
satisfyingly saturated with sweetness.

Oh, what it is to be human —
to experience all on this Earth —
this little pebble hurtling through space.

Innocence

Innocence is when
I know/sense
　　　　everything.

We lose our innocence when we
let the clamor of society override our own compass,
silence our inner knowing,
and follow our minds instead of hearts.

Let's regain our innocence,
by tuning back into ourselves...
by trusting our hearts.

We know/sense everything.

Different Pots of Gold

Not everyone searches for the same pot of gold.

Bears look for honey.

Bees seek flowers.

Where does your   r   a
                      i
                          n
                              b
                               o
                               w

                               end?

Shell of Yourself

Are you being a shell of yourself?
You worry about your looks,
how wrinkly you'll become when you're older.
You'll inject Botox into your cheeks,
like a deflated, saggy balloon
puffing itself out to fill itself with air
to reach its once plump prime.
Only your outside will be smooth and round again.
Don't be concerned with your exterior,
the surface, the facade that others see.

When you let down your guard,
take off your mask,
and wipe away your makeup,
that is when you let people see
your true beauty —
your real essence.
Your full human-ness.
You radiate joy, positivity,
hope, and wholeness.
You are *b u r ѕ t i n g*
with vivacious energy and Love.

78

You never needed to inject
extra oxygen to fix your surface
to be fuller than you are —
any bigger and you'd pop!
But your ego, your exterior,
led you to believe that you aren't enough,
that you can't be enough as you are.

Your exterior is afraid of your true greatness.
Let your self-judgments go.
Let them fall away from you
like chunks of dried red terra-cotta clay.
All that is left is your glowing,
luminescent light self,
shining with true beauty.

You are perfect exactly the way you are,
your shimmering soul in the shape of a human.
Humankind.
You are both.
Human. Kind.
You are Light.
You are Luminescent.
You are Love.

Heaven & Earth

You were born perfect
with every body part in its proper place for you.
Keep your chin up,
eyes gazing at the horizon.
They're placed up high to see Heaven,
not to stare at your feet.
Your feet ground you to the soil,
so you can achieve the perfect balance
of Heaven and Earth.

Lights On

Sometimes, we think we are

$$S$$
$$H$$
$$U$$
$$N$$
$$N$$
$$E$$
$$D$$

alone in the dark,

when we've just forgotten to open our eyes.

Home for Sale

How can you offer up a home when you aren't there,
when there is no one inside to love,
no one inside to play,
no one inside to protect?
You are a hermit crab offering to sell your own shell.
What will house you once it's gone?
What will you do once vulnerable to the sea,
without an exterior to shield you from the elements?
And for what?
A little extra wad of green fiber?
Is that worth your life, your livelihood?

You say your house is intact.
It's ready for market,
but we see it in ashes.
It burst into flames and disintegrated,
obliterated instantly before our eyes.
Re-build your nest, brick by brick,
not for us to call home, but for yourself.
Do not sell us your broken,
empty, invisible home.

Fill it with Love.
Fluff up the space.
Live in it a little first,
till it is bursting at the seams with light,
with love, radiating happiness and joy.

Fill its halls with music,
sprinkle its walls with moonlight and stardust.
Make each day a colorful party in your home.
When one can't help but smile
the second they enter its rooms.
Then and only then can you consider sharing
or giving your home to another.
Giving, not selling.
Loving, not taking.

Then and only then will your home be ready,
ripe for picking,
ripe for sharing.
Not a second before,
when it is cold, empty and dark.
When no one is home,
no shutters on the windows,
no shudders from a soul.
Nobody home.
No body here.

Heart Light Bulb

The heart is the light bulb of the soul.

It lights the cavern of your body.

Do what you love.

Speak your truth.

Be yourself—

To always brighten your home.

Tightropes

We are walking on

t
i
g
h
t
r
o
p
e
s

to our destinations.

Do not look right or left but inwards,

f
o
r

t
h
e
i
r

r
o
p
e
s

are not yours to follow.

Fiery Thoughts

There is smoke billowing
out the top of your perched pen,
like your brain stewing on high heat.
You've blown way past the simmer stage.
Like a hot, roasting oven
        with its door slightly ajar,
                        steam wafts out,
taking refuge in the cool, crisp air.

You cap your pen,
knit green hat crammed on your head,
hoping to contain your thoughts
that are leaking out the edges.
Why let them escape?!
Why are they fleeing?!
Your brain's roiling magic.
Can you turn down your brain burner,
lest you burn your boiling ideas?
Lest you allow them to evaporate
into thin, sparse, nothingness?
You breathe in deeply,
filling up your belly.
One. Two. Three...
You exhale, calming your mind,
slowing your heartbeat,
soothing your soul.

The smoke, once caustic,
now creeps out as slithering tendrils,
trickling slower and slower until suddenly —
as if a vacuum just whirred on —
it reverses direction and shoots
back into the pen in your hand,
sucked back into your brain.
Your thoughts now re-captured,
tranquilized,
move at a more manageable pace.
You breathe out a deep sigh of relief.

You take another elongated breath,
ahhhh.
Your mind quells,
calm as a crystal clear lake,
not a ripple astir.
Your head is now cleared
from its brain fog of overactivity,
over-anxiety, into peaceful equanimity.
You close your eyes,
thanking your mind for its stillness,
for allowing you to finally proceed
with jotting down your ideas onto paper,
clearing the forest of thought trees
peppering your brain,
making space for new mystical concepts to arise...

Brain Children

We birth ideas daily.
We're so prolific with our progeny,
but we often forget our own power to produce.
Each conjured thought propagates
more thoughts and realities into existence.
What kind of world do you want to live in?
Create ideas in line with that vision
so that your brain children
transform your dreams into life.

No Matter

No matter how wealthy you are,

in a drought,

you can't pay the   **sky**

           to   **w**
                  e
                  e
                  p

Faery Magic

Like faeries, we are magic incarnate.
We speak incantations with every breath.
But we've forgotten our divine power,
and think our words are empty pockets of air.
Remember you are magic to your very core.

Butterflies

A butterfly doesn't concern itself
with questions like,

Can I Fly?

After emerging from its cocoon,
it waits for its wings to dry before lifting off....

Backbends

Straighten out your back;
unbend yourself from your precarious position,
twisted sideways to carry
the burden of your brothers and sisters.
Unshackle yourself
from that old heavy cannonball
of hurt, pain, and sorrow.
That is not your own;
it was never yours to keep.
You do not need to carry it anymore.
Acknowledge it for its lesson,
for the growing pains that helped you
blossom into the beautiful being that you are.
Now, release it.

Like a rose in concrete,
you broke through the cracks,
through the walls,
through the ceiling.
You are resilient.
Anti-fragile.
Anti-fear.

Loving Yourself Into Being

Shake out your weary limbs;
allow your neck,
your spine,
your breath to elongate
back to their natural states,
back to their full, illustrious lengths.

Unfurl yourself into your wholeness.
Hold your head up high to survey your world —
your exquisite, precious world.
Blink once, twice, thrice
to observe the landscape before you change,
to shift from a barren and battered desert
into a green, glowing oasis
of love, light, joy, and peace.
This is the new world you walk into,
shoulders back,
eyes alight,
heart open,
soul soaring in the sky.

Light

If it's too dark,

lift up your shades to see the sunshine.

You control your light.

Watering Gardens

WATER

both

your & your neighbor's

gardens,

for then both

will be equally green.

Sharing

Share with others what you adore most,
not what you adore least.
The former is true love,
the latter is a facade.
If you cherish it and share it,
you know that you truly care.
You share it to nourish your soul,
to demonstrate true kindness and generosity.
To share what you don't actually want is easy;
means nothing, gives nothing—
a jar of empty air in a sea of fresh oxygen.

Nay, better to share something real,
something you love like your sweet,
honeyed voice reflecting off the rafters.
Sweet, soft music that glides
through their eardrums,
sliding into every crevice
to seek its natural home—
the heart.
The place it can't but be.

Connecting each heart together as one —
that is true joy,
true love,
true giving —
what you love that becomes another's.
That unifies all in love.
All in joy.
All in happiness.

Redwood Reflections

Meandering through the Redwood Grove,
I asked the wise one-leggeds,
"What's your secret to a long, happy life?"

    "Root down.
    Be patient.
    Stand tall.
    Adapt to changes.
    Harmonize with your neighbors.
    Breathe.
    Love."

Soda Can

When you are
about to explode,
remember that
you are a soda
can. Tap yourself
along your edges,
releasing all the
excess tension,
getting back to
your calm center.

Moon Musings

I look up at the moon,
a pearlescent sliver cloaked by clouds.
The clouds drift across until it
vanishes completely.

Was it ever really there?
Or had I just imagined it?
Do I see what I see
or what I want to see,
believe and create in my mind?
I ponder as the clouds uncover the moon again,
its light falling onto the still glass lake below.

Moon Musings II

The pearlescent half moon glows
above this still glass lake.
It's greeted by its half sister in the watery surface.
On the surface, these two moons look alike,
but one is dense, one liquid.
Half sisters that resemble twins.
However, things are not as they appear.

We think we know something when we see it,
but we're seeing our history play out again and again.
It's not the moon we see but the idea of a moon,
as we think a moon should be.
We see twin moons when one is a facade.
Don't chase the copycat for the real glow.

Caterpillar Cares

You say that you're all done,

but that's like a caterpillar saying it's a butterfly.

Be patient, and allow yourself to be...

T R A N S F O R M E D.

Falling Sky

If the sky is f
           a
            l
             l
             i
              n
               g

Catch it.

You're your own hero.

No Need to Hasten

It does not suit you to hasten,

for the joy is in the journey.

If you get there first,

with whom will you revel?

New Paths

We need not follow

    the torches of tradition.

We can light a new path,

    showing others a new way of being.

Loving Yourself Into Being

PART III

MIRACLES

Loving Yourself Into Being

BLOOM

not for anyone else's pleasure but because it was born to

A flower blossoms

Blooming

Ice Skater

You stand on ice,
feet laced up in leather ice skates.
You lift your foot to examine the fine blade
with the jagged ridges at the end.
Satisfied, you glide forward effortlessly,
arms floating at your sides.
This is not your first time on the lake.
Nor will it be your last.

A light breeze tingles along your arms,
cloaking you in a cool, wispy silver shawl.
Just the perfect temperature for skating!
You know this lake well —
every inch, every groove,
like your back jeans pocket.

The shadows of the pine trees paint the ice
in shades of gray and blue,
outlining pointy mountain ridges
on the glassy white surface.
You haven't hiked a mountain in a while.
You've stayed near what you know,
near the comfort of the ice
that predictably shifts its form
from season to season.

Loving Yourself Into Being

You prefer the ice —
water transformations over air ones:
leaves turning from green to red,
orange to crackling, dead, withered brown.

Maybe you should hike a mountain sometime,
expand the map in the corners of your mind,
sketching new contours and edges into your memory.
But what if you get lost?
Oh darling, no —
that's where the fun begins.
That's where you find yourself.

Moon Boots

Splashing in puddles,
rain boots speckled with droplets.
Stars sparkle on the watery reflection,
glinting, hinting at the magic in the galaxy.
The moon shimmers on the rippling waves
conjured up by your joyous jumps.
Heaven and Earth combine in this puddle,
as the stars nestle into the pavement.
You marvel at this miracle —
dancing on stars with moon boots
made for rainy days.

Dimples

Dimples

are   of
POTS   GOLD

    at   *rainbow*
      the   *double*
        end   *a*
          of

Laughter

Laughter is contagious.
Like a wildfire,
it burns away sorrow
and re-ignites every soul,
lighting the world anew.

s
h
e
was
mesmerized
by the moon,
  yearning to
    bathe herself
      in its luminescence.
        what a blessing;
M   seeing beauty
o   in darkness.
o
n
f
l
o
w
e
r

Transit Sunsets

The train doors open;
I step onto the platform.
Eyes transfixed,
I blink— is this a mirage?
Before me is a fiery orange sunset lighting up the sky,
setting the city on fire.

I watch this miraculous moment,
one that seems ordinary enough—mundane even—
as it happens every day, like clockwork.
But standing on this platform,
I am caught in a little snow globe of peace,
in my own little bubble,
my own little world.

I watch trains and cars pass by on either side,
people in little metal boxes on a conveyor belt
to their next check-listed item.
Like a drop of molasses plopped onto ice,
time freezes for me
while it continues for the rest of the world,
chugging along the tracks at its fast,
normal, industrialized clip.

I'm encapsulated in a hyphen —
in between time —
as other worlds glide by.
I am stuck,
rooted to the ground,
mesmerized by nature's beauty,
a silly smile plastered across my face.
I can barely breathe.
The world is on fire,
and I'm the only one watching it burn...
I watch as the glowing embers cool down —
as the city rises from the ashes.

What peace and joy exist in this world.
What beauty to behold
when one takes a moment to breathe
in the whirlwind of our lives.
Breathe in....
                    Breathe out....
There is no other place to be than here.

        Just.
                H e r e.

Word Wizard

The human touch can heal, but so can words.
These are different salves for different wounds,
salvaging body parts and soul fragments
in their respective mediums.

A word is a double-edged sword,
for it can sever or suture.
Use them carefully, impeccably,
and only ever for the highest good.

Touch is important,
but you can only be in one space at a time
(or so it is said).
Ah, but your words!
Your words can speak volumes,
carried to the highest mountain tops
or the smallest slits in the sea floor.

You can heal and transform the world,
alter perspectives just by Tetris-ing a few letters together.
Isn't THAT a miracle?
Do you know what you are?
You are a word wizard!
Wield your wand with care,
and you will conjure up magic.

Belly Button Bell

The belly button is the

$$\text{DOORBELL}$$

to the soul.

Ring it any time to remind yourself,

*"I am **here** — fully present!"*

Everyday Alchemy

You finger the soft yellow sweater,
which itself is a form of alchemy.
Turning a spool of yarn into cloth —
something to keep you warm and happy
on those cold, windy nights.
Each thread is impeccably woven
to create a magnificent, wearable piece.
One single stitch alone unravels to nothing.
It cannot be alone; it has no utility,
no meaning without being interlinked.
It yearns to be connected —
woven continuously with its fellow stitches.
Just like us, as we crave connection,
the bond that makes us human.

Not everyone finds buried treasure,
for it's not actually buried.
Some just don't see what is truly in front of them.
Treasure is yours for the taking —
it's up for your interpretation.
You make meaning out of everything,
determining the worth of every single object,
moment or being in life.

What is just a piece of clothing to another,
you know is an actual miracle:
spun, wearable gold.
What other treasures are you missing,
hidden in plain sight?

"I" Candy

Candy in a wrapper,
sweetness doled out in dollops,
easily carried in your pocket
to pass out to passersby—
A little sweetness for you, and some for you!

But we're inherently sweet enough!
Our blood flows with the sweet nectar of life;
it is in every filament of our being.
But we forget our natural honeyed presence
and think we must plop another sugar cube—
and another— into our tea.

Our sweet tooth gets sharper as we grow older,
craving more and more.
Chocolate, brownies, banana splits, creme brûlée!
But we must wean ourselves off candy crutches;
there's no missing piece to fill with Reese's pieces.
Remove the artificial sweeteners sapping us from
our own true knowing:
WE are the sweet dollop of dessert
doled out to every passerby.

Kites

Colorful kites float above your crown.

   Each one flutters right or left,

      lightly skimming over jet streams,

   bouncing playfully on wind currents.

Your kite tugs gently at your arm,

   eagerly sniffing its way in the wind,

towards the realm of clouds and rainbows.

   You loosen your rein —

      bowing, as your kite guides you to heaven. . . .

Paradise

Paradise, like a pair of dice,
derives its meaning from our interpretation.
There are only six numbers per die,
each dot innocently etched in.
But once cast, we praise or curse
the summations based on our hopes and desires.
We say it's luck,
but we choose our Heaven.
Paradise is within us.
Yet like a dealer's toss,
we say that paradise is outside our reach,
that the gods select for us.
Nay, whatever happens, happens,
and we layer on meaning
like gold wrapping paper.
We then forget that we masked the results
with our own interpretation
and think they're solid gold.

Something either happens or it doesn't,
but we slather morality over it,
liberally, like butter on toast.
But we could have easily chosen to see it differently.

That is within our control.
When we are upset with the roll of the dice,
remember it is our choice.
Life happens,
but we decide our emotions.

Rather than allow the dice to dictate your day,
you can choose paradise
every second,
every day.

Paradise lies within you, not without.

Kneading

You knead the dough, driving your palm in and out,
like a jelly fish floating in the sapphire sea.
Each thrust ripples the dough,
cascading over your palm, melting back into itself.
With each stroke, you expertly swivel the dough
a notch clockwise.

There's a certain rhythm
to this ebb and flow of dough waves.
In and out, over and back.

Your kneading is consistent,
just like you need consistency.
In an ephemeral world, shapeshifting each second,
dough rhythms remind you to slow down,
to remember the quiet, delicious moments
that heal your body and nourish your soul.

There's such magic in the "ordinary" —
transforming flour and water into bread!
Cast your desires out into the world:
whatever you need, you can knead into life,
birthing miracles with your open hands.

Flying

it's what we call…
Falling up —
You just forgot you had wings.
You're anti-gravity.
propelling you up onto your feet.
Your heart lifts you off the ground,
Catching yourself when you've hit rock bottom?

?
p
u

n
e
l
l
a
f

Have you ever

Falling Up

127

Edge Thoughts

I love sitting at the edge of a cliff,
my legs curled over the top,
like a comma,
                   poised mid-sentence —
breath abate,
the space in between what has been
and what is about to be.

My feet dangle over nothing,
walking on air,
as I gaze down over the precipice.
It's awe-inspiring feeling like an ant on a wall,
thousands of feet cascading below
and thousands of feet soaring above.
The massive expanse of the universe,
and I this minute little dot.
But the only little dot that will ever be me.

Every moment we're sitting
with our legs
                   draped
                                   over the edge.

Each future second could be our last.

But we become viscerally aware of our mortality
when we notice the steep
        d

        r

        o

        p
              right below our feet.

When life feels mundane,
trite and unending,
recall the feeling of the cool,
minty gasp in your lungs,
a quickening of your breath —
catching in your throat.
Remember the gift of being here
in this exquisite life,
and lean into
        this.
           next.
              moment...

"Hue"-man

Everything is relative.
What's tall or short,
fragile or strong,
whole or broken,
good or bad.
We live life like it's black or white,
but in doing so miss all the hues
that make us human.
We are light beings —
it's in our name,
our nature: "hue"-man.
We've just forgotten our colorful existence,
what makes us so special.
What is one person's perspective
is just one color on the spectrum,
but we think it is the literal truth.
Step back to view others' vantage points,
to see the rainbow of reasons
splashed across the world.
Acknowledge each faction of light
that creates the full spectrum of hues.

Are We in Heaven?

"Mama,
are we in heaven?"
The little boy tugs gently
at his mother's light woolen sweater,
pointing at the puffy white
clouds outside their
window.

Smiling
wistfully, she tousles
his brown, silky locks, "Heaven
is wherever you are, little
one. It is within

"Oh...
Ok...." the boy says.
He reaches out his hand towards
the plane's window, yearning
to touch those large, wispy
marshmallows.

you."

He plucks
an imaginary piece out of the air,
tucking it into his right corduroy pocket,
satisfied that he now has
some magic at his
fingertips.

131

A Cappella

Harmonize with each other —
let your voices, your souls,
vibrate in frequency.
Let your separateness dissolve,
melt away like butter on a hot burner.
Overlap your melodies
like freshly dipped wet paint
to layer yourselves gently upon one another —
orange, gold, silver, blue —
coalescing as a rainbow
on this blank canvas in our hands.

Your voices resonate and swirl together
with such a rich, lovely ombré —
amber waves cascading from your lips,
blending into each other,
into an enchanting symphony.
The air vibrates from your unity;
the walls expand,
attempting to somehow contain
the vastness of this singular magnified voice.

Nothing can hold the surge,
the tide of a harmonious melody,
a million voices woven into one.
All strands of individual silk
stitched into a stunning robe.
This is alchemy at its finest:
when gold droplets can't but drip from your lips,
into a vast ocean of love —
cloaking the Universe in Love.

Ellipses

Three dots that feel so close together
yet have infinite space between them.
If one dot wanted to feel alone, it could.
That would be accurate.
In the sea of letters in a sentence,
a paragraph, a page, a story,
one dot could get lost...
swept away in a tide of characters.

Yet, it is also true that one dot is never alone,
always threaded to the other letters
like notes in a musical ensemble.
Close or far is only relative —
because we're all related.
One note might think it's alone,
but it plays an important role when
strung together to create a magnificent symphony.

The Oatmeal Life

Life is like a bowl of oatmeal.

It starts out plain and simple.

We add any ingredients we want—

blueberries, cinnamon, nuts, milk.

We can eat all, some, or none of it.

But in the end, it is delicious,

because we made it so.

Birthing Words

The ink in my pen slithers out
onto the paper in front of me,
flowing across the page
like a dash of paint
conjoining with water,
swirling together to create a lighter,
more fluid version of its previous viscous state.

As I write, my words seep out
as if my soul was pouring honey
out of a clear glass pitcher.
It glides out smoothly, gently,
like clouds billowing over an Irish sea bluff.

These honeyed words
bathe the pancake page with warmth,
with an experienced sweetness,
like a wine that gains flavor
and deliciousness over time,
having been mulled over and over,
churned up in the barrel.

Captured in the bottle,
the red liquid, like blood,
like thoughts, simmers patiently in the brain,
poised for the perfect moment
to be birthed into fruition in this physical reality.

Leaping out of its glass cage,
the wine gushes out the neck of the bottle,
into the eager embrace of the gilded wine glass.
    Ah to breathe!
             Breathe!

The wine, the thoughts, open up to the air,
inviting the oxygen to invigorate it
into its true full-bodied nature.

Yes, the words rush out,
faster and faster now,
as they thirstily find their place on the page,
like year-long seafarers who have yearned
for sturdy land to call home.
These words spout out,
clinging to the paper
as if it were the necessary salve to their ailments.

Loving Yourself Into Being

Like a newborn pup
exhausted from its birthing journey—
eyes closed and limbs weary
from pushing outwards into existence—
the words snuggle closer to their new mother,
latching onto the white parchment,
hoping to never.
        let.
          go.

Mountain Tears

Tears are natural rivulets.

Let them run.

The mountain

does not hold back its tears.

It lets them flow,

allowing nature to bloom.

Galaxy Girl

She is the galaxy in form.
There are stars in her eyes,
rainbows coursing through her veins,
starlight dancing on her eyelids,
and moonbeams caressing her hair.
She will not apologize for her celestial self,
nor justify her own divinity.
She just beams her glorious self outwards,
welcoming others to join her in the Milky Way.

Puka Shells

We are like puka shells in an infinite loop necklace. Each shell holds and is held by the other shells, carrying each other's weight, thus becoming weightless.

Streetcar Symphony

Every day there is a symphony in the streets.
Each car is a different note.
By itself, each car looks erratic,
stopping and starting,
honking and humming.
But when we see the intricate dance of the notes
throughout the street,
oh what magical music!

Heartbeat Moments

My heartbeat pulses in my ears,
each second reverberating through my skull.
This internal tempo,
this rhythm of life,
reminds me that this moment,
this beat
       is
          all
              there
                  is.

This pulse in my finger tip pressed to my lips.
These lips that speak my truth
with every word, every breath.
This breath that flows through my body
from crown to feet.
These feet that guide me
with each step towards my future.
This future that is just my heartbeat
Now. Now. Now.

Magical Musical Conductor

A musical conductor is a magician
concocting a potion of voices
with the wave of her hand.
She extracts some soprano tendrils,
enhances alto strands,
plucks certain tenors,
wafting baritone timbres over others.
Like an alchemist,
she amalgamates disparate sounds
into one heavenly, harmonious voice.

Close Your Eyes

Close your eyes to see with your soul.

In the dark,

your heart

will guide you to the

light.

Synesthesia

Your voice paints me with honey,
each phrase stroking me with a different soft hue:
blue, green, orange, yellow.
You gently coat your colors over me,
building a masterpiece of brush strokes.

Your voice layers music upon me.
I transform into a violin.
Your voice becomes the bow,
caressing my strings with each loving bow stroke.
Different notes dance
across my face and neck as you play me,
each timbre producing a different melodious note.

Above my face appears a translucent keyboard.
Your vocal chords waltz invisibly across the piano keys,
blending harmoniously into the violin's tune.
Next, your voice layers on wind chimes,
light tinkling pings,
seamlessly intertwining into the musical symphony.
Your voice plays my back like a harp,
plucking notes on my shoulder blades,
dabbling gently along my spine.

Loving Yourself Into Being

Your voice has soft edges when you speak to me,
soft down feathers unfurling
around the rim of your vocal chords.

When you speak with others,
your voice has a glass edge,
intentionally cutting, severing others into pieces.
But with me, your voice is soft —
safe, warm, home.
Your voice envelopes me in love,
in a comforting, fluffy embrace.

When you laugh,
a beautiful, perfect red rose appears before me.
With each peal of laughter,
a petal falls softly to the ground.
This is not a wilting, sad flower;
this is a beautiful reunion —
floating petals returning to Mother Earth.

Melting Music

The music tickles my eardrums;
each note *pings* like a snowflake
falling on my cheeks,
landing softly and melting into my face,
becoming a part of me.

Who Says?

Who says we can't walk on water?

We *GLIDE* on it, no less.

What else is ice skating?

Full Bloom

Open the petals as the flower blooms;
the center is so aromatic and fresh!
The spores freshly awakened,
pure, innocent, soft to the touch.
Nothing bad has tainted them,
having not yet been exposed
to pain or suffering.
The petals' iridescent blue hue
gleams in the warm, radiant sunlight.

A smile creeps slowly across your face
as a slight breeze caresses you.
You recall the perky, earthy smell
of freshly brewed coffee
wafting from your brightly sun-kissed kitchen.
The calm Sunday mornings
where you could lazily lie in bed,
one leg poking out of the fluffy blankets,
day-dreaming about your feet in the sand
on a balmy beach.

Loving Yourself Into Being

You breathe in deeply,
filling your lungs with the ocean air,
the crashing of waves enveloping your ears
like silver curtains —
like the petals of the flower
closing back up after sunset,
covering each other for warmth and love.
You exhale happily,
releasing this remembered love
back into the world
to replenish other love-starved souls,
re-oxygenating them with lavender bliss.

The Essence of Water

You say that everything changes —
things cannot stay the same —
but my love for you never wavers.

Yes, the seasons change,
the leaves shift their colors,
and I, water, alter from snow to rain,
but my love constantly surrounds you.
I remain forever in your presence, no matter my form.
As a rainbow, an ice cube, river, or air,
I flow through you, around, above and below you.
Even if you wanted to evade me,
you could not, for you are made mostly of me.
You are filled completely with my love.

You're concerned with the here and now,
the right and wrong.
Do this, do that,
stay, don't leave;
Yes — No!
But what if you just let what is, be?
What if you could just BE
yourself,
in your fullness,
in your wholeness?

Quell your ceaseless mind for a moment.
     Om.
               Ahhhh.
Drink me in.
Let my essence soothe every cell,
every fiber of your being.
My cool, blue, clear liquid presence
heals you from the inside out.
You were never broken,
never wounded like you once believed.
You have always been whole.
You just needed a little dusting
to remove the grit that had obscured your vision
and muddied your heart.

Those permanent scars
that you believe mar your body,
are merely dirt collected upon your shell
from your experiences,
marking your triumphs,
not displaying damaged goods.
Those invisible wounds are not yours to keep.
The experiences yes,
but the pain or dirt?
No, those are for me to wash away,
to reveal your pearly opalescent skin again.

Loving Yourself Into Being

You can let them go now.
Now.
How does that feel,
to release old thoughts
that have been shackling you?
What if those were never
your thoughts to begin with?
They'd been injected into your brain by society,
brainwashing you into thinking
what is right or wrong,
good or bad,
success or failure.

You may shift form,
and as time progresses,
your exterior may alter its shape from round —
peach plump as a baby —
to strong muscled sinew to softer bones,
but your core remains pure love.
You were born to reflect this world,
to send the love that is within you outward.

At some point you forgot your purpose,
got sucked into the ephemeral winds of the world,
pulled this way and that by society.

Loving Yourself Into Being

But I am here to remind you
of your true, highest self,
never wavering in its loving radiance
for yourself and others,
emanating from your core,
without your needing to do a thing —
just by your being in this world.

Drink more of me.
Every sip sends you back to your roots,
back to your pure,
beautiful, innocent essence.
There is nothing to fear.
There is only love.
I am Love,
and thus, so are you.
For I am you.

Loving Yourself Into Being

Call a Lily

Call a Lily
by its true name:
Love.

For it is Earth's heart
offered to you
with cupped brown hands
to reflect your own pure center.

Love exudes its essence through being.
Just like you.
As you love yourself into being,
you shed false layers caked on by society —
becoming wholly yourself —
allowing others to see
the miracle that you are:

LOVE.

As you have always been
and always will be.

Loving Yourself Into Being

Thank you for reading this book, for holding my heart in your hands and allowing me to join you on your brilliant journey through life. Please know that no matter where you are in the world or when you're reading these words, I am sending you love. These pages are infused with my love, and now they are yours.

YOU are such a miracle. Thank you for making this world a better place just by being you. May you remember every day that you are enough, exactly as you are. You don't need to do or prove anything for your achievements are just the results of your behavior, not validations of your worth to society. Every small thing you do has a ripple effect on others—you have no idea how many lives you have transformed just by sharing yourself authentically! One share can change someone else's life forever. So thank you for being you.

With Love & Gratitude,
Karina Hsieh

www.karinahsieh.com
Email: thekarinahsieh@gmail.com
Instagram: @karinahsieh_

ACKNOWLEDGMENTS

A special thanks to the following people:

Karisma, Louie, Jessie & Guides
Tonia, Michael & Mason Hsieh
Heather Swallow
Leslie Bodner
Sherwood Wang
Madison Greer
Alexia Usgaard
Amanda Nguyen
Katie Mahon
Caroline Chao
Gloria Zhu
Debbie Lai
Lauren Asher
Suz Burroughs
Casey Brown
Rob Wolf Petersen
Scott Wing
Grise Hillriegel
Neekaan Oshidary
Pooja Virani
TJ Biddle
Disha Patani
Tony Molatore
Helen Yang
Rebekah Moan
Hunter Franks

You have each helped make this
poetry collection possible, and I am so
grateful you're in my life!

ABOUT THE AUTHOR

Karina Hsieh grew up in Oakland, California. She
studied Psychology at Harvard and worked as a
"Happiness Engineer" in Silicon Valley before
backpacking solo around the world for 1-1/2 years
to cultivate her own self-love and compassion.
She craves exponential growth and perpetually
follows Love, especially self-love, as her North
Star. When she's not writing, you can find her
dancing, singing, traveling, teaching fitness classes,
or unmasking miracles hidden in plain sight.